Trap

Pass

Move

Coach Dad's Guide
to Better Soccer

Trap
Pass
Move

Coach Dad's Guide to Better Soccer
Youth Soccer Training, Drills & Games

By

Jeff Kight

Jeff Kight

Published by White Dog Publishing

The contents of this book are drawn from the experiences of the author. Many of the drills, games and training concepts included are common throughout youth coaching. Most included here have been modified from generic training practices to fit the authors needs.

Extensive efforts have been made to make sure that no intellectual property has been infringed upon in the writing of this book.

Any questions may be directed to the author at TPM@jeffkight.com

ISBN: 978-1-4837-0713-6

1 2 3 4 5 6 7 8 9 10

Trap - Pass - Move

Content

Thank you

to all of the players and parents

who made coaching a pleasure.

Thank you

to my boys Caleb & Jesse

who allowed me to be their coach.

A special thank you

to my wife Christine

who allowed me to play.

Caleb preparing for another *"Zlatan Moment"*.

He's developed into an intelligent and
talented rock, able to control the field
from Keeper to Striker.

Jesse...*la pulga*...one of the softest touches
on the field and best distributors around.

He may dance around the opponent
or muscle right through - whatever is needed.

Jeff Kight

Forward

I did it all wrong. Well, maybe not all wrong but if I started coaching u6 and u8 players today my entire system would be different.

Ten years ago I started helping coach my oldest son in soccer mainly because his coach knew virtually nothing about the sport. He was a dad like me our difference was that I enjoyed the game and had some history playing.

Before I get started I must applaud all Dads & Moms who step up and become involved in coaching or otherwise helping with a team especially when they know little or nothing about the game. Appreciation must also be given to organizations who promote soccer and sports in general and help teach parents the games their children play. AYSO in particular has exceptional training programs for coaches, referees and players unfortunately few take full advantage of everything available.

Our experience with club soccer is as hit and miss as with any organized youth sport, it all depends on the coach and great, passionate coaches are few and far between. And if there is no required training for coaches within an organization there can be a large divide between the top teams and those at the bottom.

As coaches we must continually learn ways to inspire our players and build stronger teams. What we did at u10 does not generally work at u14. We must adapt, grow, learn just as we ask our players to do.

We're all busy and taking courses and looking up drills and information online is time consuming. That's why I've written this booklet, to put a decade of being Coach Dad into one place. I've boiled a lot of information and experience down in hopes that it will save you time and help you avoid the mistakes I made in the beginning.

Introduction

Soccer is a young sport, Futbal on the other hand has a long and rich history spanning the globe. The game as played and especially trained in the United States differs from that in South America and Europe. But then the Germans style of play differs from the Brazilians and the English from the Portuguese. Each country or region infuses its natural flare into the game.

The turning point in my coaching and the enjoyment of our players and winning of our team came when we started to incorporate more international training methods. It seems obvious now, simply look at countries that consistently produce exceptional teams and train like they do.

In the United States we have adopted a belief that participation is to be rewarded and winning ignored. We give trophies and medals to everyone for a "good job" creating a lack of desire to become better, to work and sweat to excel. The rest of the world will tell you you're not good enough, they will celebrate their win and morn their loss only to train better in order to win the next game.

There is certainly some good to be learned from a loss but not a lot from simply participating.

Let's face it, at u6 maybe kids aren't sure who won but past that they know if they're team stinks or not. Why sugar coat rancid meat? Just work harder, train smarter, have fun and get better.

Before anyone gets the wrong idea I'm not some win at all costs, all that matters is winning type. Actually, I have told my teams over the years that I'd rather see them play well and get progressively better than win. Sometimes even your best is not good enough to win but if you play well and progress in your skills one day you may be 'the best'.

In the following pages I have compiled some of my training methods and drills and the philosophies behind each. They are rooted in what I now believe to be a great system of training to produce excited, progressively better players and team.

In case you are wondering; Yes we see huge leaps in player skills in the game; Yes we see better team play; Yes we win. I attribute these things to how we now train.

Chapter 1

Planting Seeds

I was talking to a Coach Dad the other day and he shared the same story I've heard for years. His daughter plays u8 soccer and the team needed a coach so he stepped up. While many times I hear "...and I know nothing about soccer." he actually did know the game and played on an indoor adult team. His main issue was a lack of time to give to developing a practice schedule and while he had an assistant coach he had zero soccer knowledge.

In his words his team was comprised of "One kid who has a clue, three who kind of get it and the rest who are lost."

Sound familiar? At u8 if you have one who "gets it" you should feel fortunate.

So how does a coach with a busy

schedule plan and run a practice? Usually they pick up one or two drills from a web site or another coach or an organization email. They incorporate these with a scrimmage, perhaps attempt to toss in a bit of theory or tactics (rarely) and call it a practice. Oh yeah, they run laps.

The thing that most coaches at this level don't understand is that the mental development children allows for limited comprehension and slower, single dimensional processing.

What does that mean?

Remember u6 games? 3v3 with a pack of all six players in a group kicking at and following the ball. Oh, there are always one or two kids who didn't like to be in the crowd so they'd stand to the side and watch. Occasionally you find a player, usually one who with older athletic siblings, who understood that eventually the ball would pop out of the pack and he could grab it and run freely to the goal. They were the stars.

The point is, the 4-5 year old can focus on one thing, the ball. They are oblivious to where their teammates are, that it was their teammate that they just stole the ball from, and that soccer is a game of passing and space.

It's a little better at u8 but it's not until they are 10, 11, even 12 that they are able to process ball-team-mate-defender-pass and it's not until early teens that the concept of playing in space is understood. This does not mean you can't address it but don't get frustrated when your 7 year olds don't run a give-n-go flawlessly.

The way I introduced concepts such as passing into space was to plant a seed.

"I'm going to plant a seed in your mind." I'd say. "You may not understand it now but in a few years you'll be playing and poof it will hit you and you'll understand. You'll say *'That's what coach was talking about.'*"

Who knows, that seed may germinate faster because of when it was planted.

19

Whether you're a Coach Dad with no knowledge of soccer or a seasoned pro it's important to remember that the kids just want to play. They want to have fun and it's our job as coaches to create practices that allow them to become better players, understand the game and perhaps most of all learn to be better people. That includes understanding the rewards of work.

Tips:

- Plant a lot of seeds.

- Don't get frustrated when "They just don't get it."

- Tell them that you are planting a seed and it's OK if they don't understand at that moment. It eases any worry they may have when they don't understand.

Chapter 2

Why and How I Did It Wrong

As a beginning coach my assumption was that the kids playing wanted to play and learn soccer. I believed that they would think about soccer at home, practice soccer at home, watch soccer at home...WRONG!

For the most part the players I've coached over the years would rather have been playing video games or watching TV or doing almost anything other than running and kicking a ball. Many did like sports, most, especially at the early ages, were 'forced' to play a sport "to get some exercise" so they tried soccer. It was my personal goal to make soccer lovers out of every one by making practices fun while teaching them the skills of the game and the meaning of team.

A few were converted, most still couldn't care less.

That the kids don't want to be professional soccer players is not a bad thing it was simply frustrating to see a kid with raw talent prefer to play on an electronic device than progress his skills.

For those who were interested in getting better I believe I could have helped more by what we focused on in practice at earlier ages. What was taught in practice was useful but perhaps presented backward.

From the time I decided to coach to today I spend time researching soccer, and now futsal, to find better and more fun ways to teach the skills used in soccer. From mental development in children to push passes I've read and watched videos, attended other teams practices and talked to a neurophycologist friend all to help develop practice sessions that would build a team while keeping players interested.

Ten years later I can see the results of

this process in the players I've coached throughout those years.

Today I continue to research however, I have begun to look not at the drills used but into the methods and processes used to train players in Europe and in particular South America.

I did it backward.

In the early days my focus was primarily on training team. I drilled set pieces, quick play, knowing where to be in circumstances like a corner kick or a throw in. Much of the time we were the team who looked like they knew what they were doing. The players had a blueprint and followed it.

Space and movement were introduced at earlier ages but not pursued, I simply 'Planted a seed'. Player mental development is not enough at six to fully understand the concept of playing in space or pass and move, focus is on 'ball!' and their immediate surroundings.

As seasons came and went my training followed the blueprint method, introducing new elements based on age and player capacity to grasp the underlying concept. Today we have a very good team filled with close friends but..........

Remember when I said that I believed that players would practice at home. I learned they won't. Most won't. 99.99% of players won't practice at home. Yeah, that's a number derived from scientific studies of millions of kids playing soccer in the United States under the age of ten.

Not really, but I'm sticking with it.

It's important to remember that most of the kids who play soccer, who play most sports, at early ages are exploring, they want to play something or their parents want them to play something and soccer is one of the *somethings*. Many will play only a few years then find they prefer baseball or basketball or chess. (Remind me to talk about chess later, it's an excellent mental development tool).

Even so, I believe that through better training at earlier ages we will be able to keep more of the excellent athletes in soccer and not have them playing other sports. Generating more interest in the beautiful game will help promote it thereby raising our world presence.

So how do we do this?

In looking at other countries young player development, especially that of South American countries where much of the development is on the streets, I see more focus on individual player, not team play, coaching.

Certainly there must be an understanding of the game, flow and 'where you need to be' but the majority of the focus is on the individual skills.

If we look at the Pareto Principle, the 80-20 rule, what 20% of play makes up 80% of soccer?

Trap – Pass – Move

Trap – It is extremely important for

a player to have control of the ball on his first touch. Whether it's a simple foot stop from a short pass or chest trap from a long cross players must be able to stop or direct the ball with command. Balls that bounce six feet away from the player are most often lost.

Pass – Accurate passing is one element necessary in successful soccer and a beginning point for new and young players. Quick passes involve mental development and come at older ages, 9-11, and quick, accurate passes with a move following is the next step.

Move – Soccer is a fluid game with constant movement. While young players tend to kick the ball then watch the action planting the seed of pass then move is important for quicker game comprehension.

—————————

At early ages, 4-6 we are primarily developing foot-eye coordination. The more robust the **Trap – Pass** training is at this age the easier it is for players to develop fancy tricks at 8-10.

While dribbling the ball is certainly an important element of soccer it is far less important to train at younger ages. Kids dribble naturally. I remember chasing my youngest son pretending to be the Soccer Monster as he kicked the ball laughing. His legs were so short at two years old that he looked like Messi controlling the ball. It never rolled more than a step away not because of his skill but because of his lack of strength.

Young kids are natural dribblers, train trapping and passing more, dribbling less. Just look at the pros....

- A Journal of Sports Sciences study of 30 French League 1 matches found that:

- The total distance covered by these professional players was slightly more than 11km per match (nearly 7 miles).

- Players had, on average, 47 possessions per match.

- Of the 11km covered, only 191m was run with the ball.

- This translates into about 53 sec of the match spent in possession of the ball.

- During each possession, the player covered 3-5m.

- The player held on to the ball for slightly more than one second.

- Each player averaged two touches per possession.

I know, these are pros and we're coaching kids but still, if we are preparing our players to play soccer shouldn't we teach them the skills that will better prepare them for higher levels, say u14?

Dribbling is such a small portion of soccer and yet is comprises large sections of time during practices, mainly because it is easy to set up a few cones in a row and have players slalom through them for fifteen minutes. Quite easy for a coach, not so much fun for a 6 year old.

I confess, I used dribbling drills a lot. Can't say that years later I have many players with exceptional control because of it.

So what should we be doing early on? We should be using drills that incorporate passing, trapping and moving. At u6 test the 'moving' out or introduce it later in the season and focus on passing and trapping along with fun 'games' that incorporate moving and dribbling.

Tips:

- Plant more seeds.

- Tell your players stories of pro soccer players.

- Allow them to be creative. Give them a few 'fancy' moves and time to play with one they like during each practice. This is what they will show Mom & Dad and be excited about.

Jeff Kight

Chapter 3

1,000,000 Touches

This is a good time to introduce the concept of 1,000,000 touches.

A coach friend introduced this to me and while it is a bit analytical for my mind, counting touches, **touches = progress**, I do agree that the more time your foot is on a ball the more likely you will increase your skill.

One million touches looks like a lot but when broken down if you get in 550 touches per day for five years you have over a million. In cultures where futball is life this is easily reachable. In the U.S. we need to make an effort. In an average practice we counted that our touch per player during our 1 hr. 30 min. was in the 350 range at u14. Once we made an attempt to increase touches we easily drove this to over

2000. Simply by starting practice with easy warm-ups that focused on small touches; toe touches, tic-tocs, juggles, roll overs, etc. moving then to short passing & volley drills we significantly increased each players touches on the ball. These 'warm-ups' took less than 30 minutes, totaled more than 1,000 touches and focused on ball control.

With effort and planning it would be easy to increase touches during any practice at any age by 200%+ and more at older ages.

Do additional touches equal better players? I don't know but I believe that more quality touches do. Design your practices around fundamental skills, the 20% that makes the 80%, with more quality touches and your players will become better.

Tips:

• Remind your players that pros run through a similar warm-up before games and practices. We routinely see them doing small touch drills on TV.

- Add creative moves to your touch warm-ups so players learn different skills and don't get bored doing the same thing over and over.

- For a great 'touch' workout look for the 1,000 Touch Workout at JeffKight.com/trap-pass-move.

Jeff Kight

Chapter 4

U10-12

Coaching gets interesting at the u10 level. Kids are beginning to understand more about the game. Their minds are developing so concepts are starting to make sense. It's not just "Kick the ball!" anymore. You're also seeing more players who want to be there and fewer "My mom makes me play." kids. Oh, you still get those or the kids who prefer watching planes or searching for four leaf clovers, probably so they can make a wish to be playing Minecraft instead of soccer.

If your kid is one of these, or if you coach a couple, getting them more excited about playing can generate more interest. That's the whole goal of this book, to get young players better faster so they are not the 'loser' on the team and your team is not the pushover of the league. We want our players playing well and feeling great about their time spent playing. They'll have more fun that way and so will you.

KEY ELEMENT – How likely are players to run up when you pick them up after practice and yell excitedly "Mom, Dad, look at the corner kick play we learned today!" or "Watch me pass the ball!"

They won't.

The excitement for passing, trapping and knowing what to do when comes in games, after wins. The excitement after practice, and OOOOHHH YEAH! generating excitement for practice, comes with the fun & fancy moves we sprinkle in along with the core 20%.

I cannot stress enough training the core 20%, **Trapping – Passing – Moving**. By focusing on these skills you will be building competent, confident players and a strong team. But to generate more individual excitement sprinkling in a few fancies will help.

Every practice take 15 minutes to let your players practice juggling, teach them an easy move, remember that at this age simple pace & direction change moves make a huge impact. Here are a few easy favorites:

Elastico – Dribble toward a cone (defender), push the ball out with a soft touch. Roll your foot around the ball so the inside of your foot is touching the ball then flick the ball in the opposite direction.

Cruyff Turn – Cock your leg as if to shot or give a strong kick then pull the ball behind your plant foot with your kicking foot.

Sissors – Touch the ball out softly then step out wide around the ball. You can then drag the ball with the inside of the other foot in one direction or flick it in the other with the outside of the foot.

Rivelino – Pretend to pass or shoot with one foot circling your foot around the ball instead of contacting it. Then flick the ball in the opposite direction with the same foot.

At this age five is enough fancy tricks to introduce. You'll find that 2-3 are favorites and become the ones most players focus on. These are primarily designed to excite players and give them a sense of WOW, something they can take home and show mom, dad, the dog and friends. It's also giving them more time on the ball and increasing touches.

Tips:

- Fancy moves excite young players but remember that the 20% make better players.

- Teach Pace and Direction Change. These are the two most valuable 'skills' a player can use to lose a defender.

- Incorporate one or two easier fancies in your Touch Warmup.

- For a great 'touch' workout and other moves look for the 1,000 Touch Workout at JeffKight.com/trap-pass-move.

Chapter 5

Communication

One of the most difficult things to get young soccer players to do is to talk. Talk on the field that is. Talking during practice is something a coach must expect. To promote on the field communication remember to include it in drills.

When doing passing drills make sure to remind players to call for the ball as a cue for a pass to be made. You can also reverse this and have the passer call the name of the receiver. This will help to build communication on both ends of the play and help condition young players to talk constructively.

This is also a good age to introduce terms and concepts like "Through!", 'Drop.", and "Down." These are all Pass & Move communications that build upon your practices. Players will now see *whys* to what they've been training.

Tips:

- Let your team make up their own code words for various runs or plays. I know a coach who uses Banana for an offside trap. It's fun and opponents won't know what's going on.

Chapter 6

Weekly Practice Schedules

U6

At ages 4 & 5 games rather than drills work best. You'll probably have a single one hour practice each week so make it fun with a couple water breaks. You will need to work on the basic *How To-When To*:

How to do a proper throw in – When to do a throw in.

What is a Goal Kick and when to do it.

What is a Corner Kick and when to do it.

How to do a Kickoff.

Don't handle the ball.

Remind them of these each practice and incorporate small touch drills that increase foot-on-ball time.

Warm-up

5-10 minutes   Every Practice

Toe Touches – 20x

Tic-Tocs – 20x

Push Out-Pull In – 10 per foot. With the outside of the foot push the ball out then roll it back in with the sole of the foot. The ball should travel about one rotation and stay within leg reach. Alternate sides.

Passing & Trapping

15 minutes   Every Practice

Pair players and place them 3-5 yards apart. Have them pass the ball back and forth. You're looking for passing accuracy, technique (this is a push pass not a toe kick but at this age the toe is most likely what you'll see) and trapping. Incorporate a futsal style trap using the sole of the foot as well as a soccer trap using the inside of the foot. Remind them that they have two feet and encourage them to pass and trap with each.

Pirates (aka Sharks & Minnows and others)

15-20 minutes   Rotating game

Mark off an area about 20 yards x 20 yards.

Each player needs a ball on his foot except one, the Pirate whose job it is to steal each player's ball and kick it out of bounds. Once a player's ball has been 'lost' he also becomes a Pirate.

This drill teaches ball control, movement, avoidance of a defender. It also works on taking the ball from an opponent and once there are multiple Pirates team defending.

Encourage the Pirates to work together as a unit focusing on a player with the ball not to go about the area willy-nilly chasing separate players.

The Numbers Game

15-20 minutes   Rotating game

Split your team into two even teams. Have each team stand next to separate goals. Give each player on each team a number. I like to match like skilled players giving them the same number.

You now stand to the side with the ball. Toss the ball into the field of play as you yell a number.

That number player from each team runs to the ball. The first one to the ball starts attacking, the other defending. If the defender steals the ball he now attacks and the other defends. The object is to score.

If the ball is kicked out of bounds or a shot is missed the session is over.

Time to toss a ball and call another set of numbers.

As time progresses call one number, wait then call another. At the end I'll start calling numbers until everyone is in the action.

Scrimmage

15-20 minutes

Kids love to scrimmage. As they do look for the concepts you've been training in practices. Praise any that you see.

U8

At 6 & 7 games are still important as are the How To-When To mentioned previously but more drills can be introduced.

The first few practices I always liked to line all the players up shoulder to shoulder, with space between each, and have each do a proper Throw In. Everyone watches technique as well as how far the player throws the ball.

Do the same with kicking the ball. You're wanting to know how well they throw/kick and for the entire team to see how far each player can throw and kick!

"See how far he can throw/kick the ball?" I'd ask. "Now if I'm all the way on the other side of the field yelling 'I'm open! I'm open!' is he going to be able to throw/kick the ball go me before an opponent getting it?"

"No." everyone would answer.

I used this all the way up to u14.

You'll probably have two one hour to

one and a half hour practice each week so make it fun. Use small touch drills as warm-ups to increase foot-on-ball time.

Warm-up

15 minutes   Every Practice

Toe Touches – 20

Tick-Tocks – 20

Push Out-Pull In – 10 per foot

Roll Overs – 10x each direction per foot

Juggles – 20x. No they don't have to juggle it 20 times in a row, the ball can hit the ground. Just have them drop the ball and kick it back waist high and catch it. This is a great way to learn to juggle.

Passing & Trapping

15 minutes   Every Practice

Pair players and place them 5-7 yards apart. Have them pass the ball back and forth. You're looking for passing accuracy, technique (this is a push pass not a toe kick) and trapping. Incorporate a futsal style trap using the sole of the foot as well as a soccer trap using the inside of the foot. Remind them that they have two feet and encourage them to pass and trap with each.

Have the passing player call the name of his intended target.

Midway through the drill have one line take three steps backward expanding the distance between the pairs.

Variation of Passing & Trapping

15 minutes   Every Practice

Divide players into 3s and place them 3-5 yards apart. The player in the middle will have no ball, the other two will have a ball.

The middle player will face one mate and call "Ball" the player will pass the ball to the middle player who will one or two touch it back. The middle player will quickly turn to face his other partner and call "Ball" repeating the receive/pass sequence. He will continue to repeat the call-receive-pass back 10 times (coach sets the # per side) on each side then be replaced by one of the outside players.

Once all players in the trio have completed 20 receive/pass back (10 per side) the process can be repeated with volley passes if desired.

This drill not only builds trap-pass but incorporates communication.

Pass & Move

15 minutes   Alternate w/other passing drills

Set out four cones about five yards apart in a square. Group players in 3s having them stand at a cone in the square. Yes, one cone will have no player on it. You'll need one ball per trio.

The player with the ball will pass to the empty cone as the 'free' player adjacent to the empty cone runs in and receives the ball. He then turns and passes to the cone he vacated as the next adjacent player runs and receives.

The ball is always passed to the empty cone and a player always runs to that cone to receive the pass.

This is a drill that works passing, trapping & moving, teaching passing to a spot where a player WILL be not to the player himself. This is an introduction to playing in space.

Pirates (aka Sharks & Minnows and others)

15 minutes   Rotating game

Mark off an area about 20 yards x 20 yards.

Each player needs a ball on his foot except one, the Pirate whose job it is to steal each player's ball and kick it out of bounds. Once a player's ball has been 'lost' he also becomes a Pirate.

This drill teaches ball control, movement, avoidance of a defender. It also works on taking the ball from an opponent and once there are multiple Pirates team defending.

Encourage the Pirates to work together as a unit focusing on a player with the ball not to go about the area willy-nilly chasing separate players.

British Bulldogs

This is not my favorite practice activity but I still have players beg to play British Bulldogs. It's better than running laps, which players moan about, because it consists of more soccer like running...sprints & rests.

Line your players up on one side of the eighteen box or a large marked off area. Put one 'Bulldog' in the center. The object is for players to run from one side of the box to the other without being tagged or going outside the lines.

The Bulldog counts down "One! Two! Three!"

The runners yell "British Bulldog!" and begin running.

If tagged that player immediately becomes a Bulldog.

Continue running players back and forth until the last has been tagged. Now he's the Bulldog.

A variation of this is to have players dribble from side to side having to avoid the Bulldog who must kick their ball out of bounds.

The Numbers Game

15 minutes   Rotating game

Split your team into two even teams. Have each team stand next to separate goals. Give each player on each team a number. I like to match like skilled players giving them the same number.

You now stand to the side with the ball. Toss the ball into the field of play as you yell a number.

That number player from each team runs to the ball. The first one to the ball starts attacking, the other defending. If the defender steals the ball he now attacks and the other defends. The object is to score.

If the ball is kicked out of bounds or a shot is missed the session is over.

Time to toss a ball and call another set of numbers.

As time progresses call one number, wait then call another. At the end I'll start calling numbers until everyone in in the action.

Scrimmage

5-20 minutes

U10-12

At the beginning of the season re-member the How Far Can He Throw/Kick drill mentioned in u8. This is a great reminder for everyone and a good way for you to see how well players understand the process of a throw-in and strong kick.

Warm-up

Every Practice

Have a few balls lined up where your players enter the field. Tell them the first thing they do when they arrive is to do the touch warm-up. This will save practice time and allow each player to learn to manage himself.

Toe Touches – 50

Tick-Tocks – 50

Push Out-Pull In – 25 per foot

Roll Overs – 25x each direction per foot

Juggles – 50x. No they don't have to juggle it 20 times in a row, the ball can hit the ground. Just have them drop the ball and kick it back waist high and catch it. This is a great way to learn to juggle.

Touch Passing & Volley

20 minutes   Every Practice

Divide players into 3s and place them 3-5 yards apart. The player in the middle will have no ball, the other two will have a ball.

The middle player will face one mate and call "Ball" the player will pass the ball to the middle player who will one or two touch it back. The middle player will quickly turn to face his other partner and call "Ball" repeating the receive/pass sequence. He will continue to repeat the call-receive-pass back 10 times (coach sets the # per side) on each side then be replaced by one of the outside players.

Once all players in the trio have completed 20 receive/pass back (10 per side) the process can be repeated with inside of the foot volley passes then top of the foot volley passes then chest to volley passes.

This drill not only builds trap-pass but incorporates communication.

Pass & Move

15 minutes   Rotate with other passing drills

Set out four cones about five yards apart in a square. Group players in 3s having them stand at a cone in the square. Yes, one cone will have no player on it. You'll need one ball per trio.

The player with the ball will pass to the empty cone as the 'free' player adjacent to the empty cone runs in and receives the ball. He then turns and passes to the cone he vacated as the next adjacent player runs and receives.

The ball is always passed to the empty cone and a player always runs to that cone to receive the pass.

This is a drill that works passing, trapping & moving, teaching passing to a spot where a player WILL be not to the player himself. This is an introduction to playing in space.

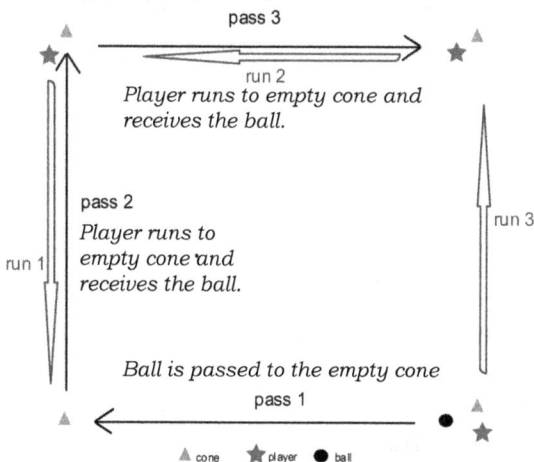

pass 3

run 2

Player runs to empty cone and receives the ball.

pass 2

Player runs to empty cone and receives the ball.

run 1

run 3

Ball is passed to the empty cone

pass 1

▲ cone ★ player ● ball

Cris-Cross Passing & Receiving

15-20 minutes   Rotate with other passing drills

There are two variations of this that I use both confuse players at first but both help their receiving and passing on the move. Try these with your u10 team but it may be better suited for

55

u12 and above.

Version One

Put four cones out in a square. Diagonal cones should be 15-20 yards apart depending on your age group.

Put one cone in the middle. This represents the 'defender'.

Split your team evenly between the four cones making the square. They will be moving diagonally through the square not along the exterior.

Give a ball to two nonfacing lines.

The player facing a player with a ball runs to the center cone rounding that cone and calling for the ball. The player with the ball passes to his teammate who is rounding the cone, receives the ball, turns back toward his original line and passes to the next person.

Now the original passer runs to the center cone calling for the ball as he rounds the cone, receives then passes to the next person in line.

Each 'receiver' goes to the end of his

respective line.

This sounds easy enough however, as both pairs of lines start going congestion occurs at the center cone, something players must account for.

This drill trains, receiving while moving, controlling the ball, passing and

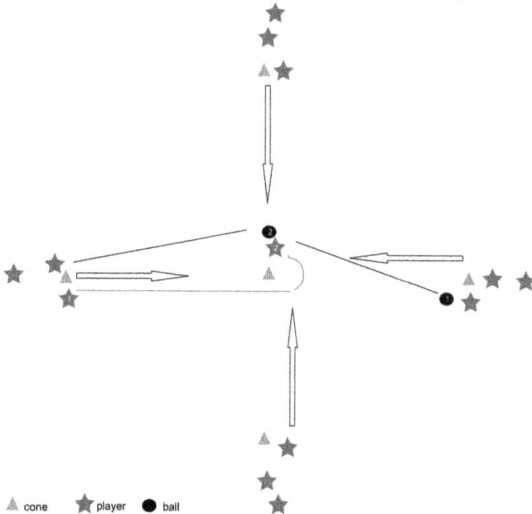

△ cone ★ player ● ball

Player (1) runs to and rounds the center cone (pretend it's a defender) calling for the ball on the opposite side of the cone (2). Player receives the ball, turns and passes to the next in his line. This repeats alternating sides in BOTH directions.

keeping your eyes up to avoid a collision.

Version Two

Put four cones out in a square. Diagonal cones should be 20-25 yards apart depending on your age group.

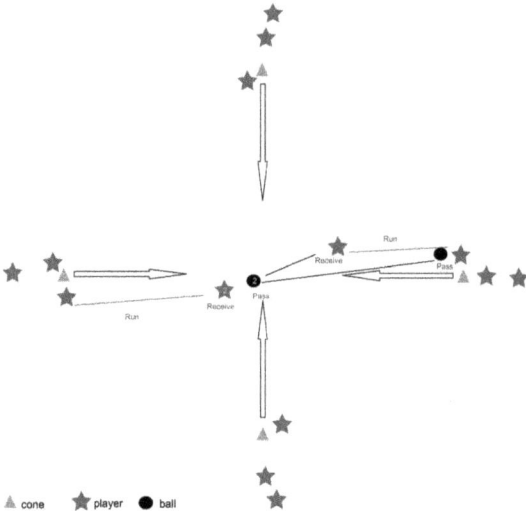

cone *player* *ball*

Player runs toward the center of the cones calling for the ball. Player receives the ball on the run them passes to the facing player who is running toward him. This repeats alternating sides in BOTH directions. Highlights receiving oncoming ball, control and accurate passing in traffic.

Split your team evenly between the four cones making the square. They will be moving diagonally through the square not along the exterior.

Give a ball to two nonfacing lines.

The person with the ball starts dribbling, small touches only. His facing partner moves in his direction.

The player with the ball passes to the oncoming teammate who receives the ball controls it then passes to the next player in the facing line.

This drill works on passing, receiving while moving toward the ball and quick control-pass while moving in a tight space.

Yes, each pair of lines go at once causing congestion in the middle of the area. Remind players to keep their head up and watch for other players and balls.

The Numbers Game

15-20 minutes   Rotating game

Split your team into two even teams.

Have each team stand next to separate goals. Give each player on each team a number. I like to match like skilled players giving them the same number.

You now stand to the side with the ball. Toss the ball into the field of play as you yell a number.

That number player from each team runs to the ball. The first one to the ball starts attacking, the other defending. If the defender steals the ball he now attacks and the other defends. The object is to score.

If the ball is kicked out of bounds or a shot is missed the session is over.

Time to toss a ball and call another set of numbers.

As time progresses call one number, wait then call another. At the end I'll start calling numbers until everyone in in the action.

British Bulldogs

15 minutes Rotating game

This is not my favorite practice activity but I still have players beg to play British Bulldogs. It's better than running laps, which players moan about, because it consists of more soccer like running...sprints & rests.

Line your players up on one side of the eighteen box or a large marked off area. Put one 'Bulldog' in the center. The object is for players to run from one side of the box to the other without being tagged or going outside the lines.

The Bulldog counts down "One! Two! Three!"

The runners yell "British Bulldog!" and begin running.

If tagged that player immediately becomes a Bulldog.

Continue running players back and forth until the last has been tagged. Now he's the Bulldog.

A variation of this is to have players dribble from side to side having to avoid the Bulldog who must kick their ball out of bounds.

Offense v Defense

20-30 minutes

Divide your team into offense and defense. Yes, use defenders on defense and attackers on offense. Let players work on their skillsets in practice.

Have the goalkeeper punt the ball so that the attackers can practice controlling a punt/long kick.

The object is for attack to score or defense kick the ball over the midfield line.

If you have enough players use your defensive midfielders in front of the defense for higher pressure and use them behind attack for support.

Encourage lateral movement for attackers, drops to support players, overlaps and through balls.

On defense work on starting wide and compressing as attack moves in. Defense must move as a unit creating an umbrella around the eighteen box.

Use 1-2-3 defending to enforce team

defending and train players not to 'dive in' at the ball.

Scrimmage

15-30 minutes

The scrimmage has always been our team's favorite activity. It's play! We traditionally end every practice with a scrimmage During which I'm looking for the skills and concepts we practiced that day.

U14+

Warm-up

Every Practice

Have a few balls lined up where your players enter the field. Tell them the first thing they do when they arrive is to do the touch warm-up. This will save practice time and allow each player to learn to manage himself.

Toe Touches – 100

Tick-Tocks – 100

Push Out-Pull In – 50 per foot

Roll Overs – 50x each direction per foot

Juggles – 100x. No they don't have to juggle it 20 times in a row, the ball can hit the ground. Just have them drop the ball and kick it back waist high and catch it. This is a great way to learn to juggle.

Touch Passing & Volley

30 minutes   Every Practice

Divide players into 3s and place them

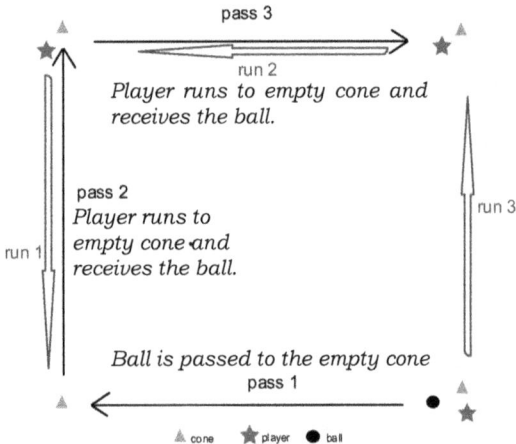

pass 3

run 2

Player runs to empty cone and receives the ball.

pass 2

Player runs to empty cone and receives the ball.

run 1

run 3

Ball is passed to the empty cone

pass 1

▲ cone   ★ player   ● ball

3-5 yards apart. The player in the middle will have no ball, the other two will have a ball.

The middle player will face one mate and call "Ball" the player will pass the ball to the middle player who will one or two touch it back. The middle player will quickly turn to face his other partner and call "Ball" repeating the receive/pass sequence. He will continue to repeat the call-receive-pass back 10 times (coach sets the # per side) on each side then be replaced by one of the outside players.

Once all players in the trio have completed 20 receive/pass back (10 per side) the process can be repeated with inside of the foot volley passes then top of the foot volley passes then chest to volley passes.

This drill not only builds trap-pass but incorporates communication.

Cris-Cross Passing & Receiving

15-20 minutes   Alternate w/other
                                 passing drills

There are two variations of this that I use both confuse players at first but both help their receiving and passing on the move. Try these with your u10 team but it may be better suited for u12 and above.

Version One

Put four cones out in a square. Diagonal cones should be 15-20 yards apart depending on your age group.

Put one cone in the middle. This represents the 'defender'.

Split your team evenly between the four cones making the square. They will be moving diagonally through the square not along the exterior.

Give a ball to two non-facing lines.

The player facing a player with a ball runs to the center cone rounding that cone and calling for the ball. The player with the ball passes to his teammate who is rounding the cone, receives the ball, turns back toward his original line and passes to the next person.

Now the original passer runs to the center cone calling for the ball as he rounds the cone, receives then passes to the next person in line.

Each 'receiver' goes to the end of his respective line.

This sounds easy enough however, as both pairs of lines start going congestion occurs at the center cone, something players must account for.

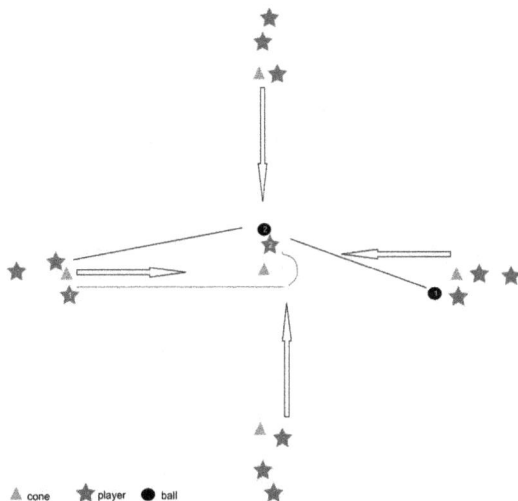

Player (1) runs to and rounds the center cone (pretend it's a defender) calling for the ball on the opposite side of the cone (2). Player receives the ball, turns and passes to the next in his line. This repeats alternating sides in BOTH directions.

This drill trains, receiving while moving, controlling the ball, passing and keeping your eyes up to avoid a collision.

Version Two

Put four cones out in a square. Diagonal cones should be 20-25 yards apart depending on your age group.

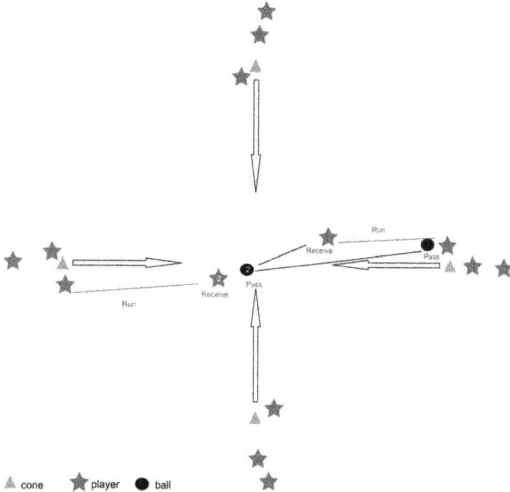

Player runs toward the center of the cones calling for the ball. Player receives the ball on the run them passes to the facing player who is running toward him. This repeats alternating sides in BOTH directions. Highlights receiving oncoming ball, control and accurate passing in traffic.

Split your team evenly between the four cones making the square. They will be moving diagonally through the square not along the exterior.

Give a ball to two non-facing lines.

The person with the ball starts dribbling, small touches only. His facing partner moves in his direction.

The player with the ball passes to the oncoming teammate who receives the ball controls it then passes to the next player in the facing line.

This drill works on passing, receiving while moving toward the ball and quick control-pass while moving in a tight space.

Yes, each pair of lines go at once causing congestion in the middle of the area. Remind players to keep their head up and watch for other players and balls.

Offense v Defense

20-30 minutes

Divide your team into offense and

defense. Yes, use defenders on defense and attackers on offense. Let players work on their skill sets in practice.

Have the goalkeeper punt the ball so that the attackers can practice controlling a punt/long kick.

The object is for attack to score or defense kick the ball over the midfield line.

If you have enough players use your defensive midfielders in front of the defense for higher pressure and use them behind attack for support.

Encourage lateral movement for attackers, drops to support players, overlaps and through balls.

On defense work on starting wide and compressing as attack moves in. Defense must move as a unit creating an umbrella around the eighteen box.

Use 1-2-3 defending to enforce team defending and train players not to 'dive in' at the ball.

Scrimmage

15-30 minutes

The scrimmage has always been our team's favorite activity. It's play! We traditionally end every practice with a scrimmage During which I'm looking for the skills and concepts we practiced that day.

These are not all of the drills and activities we've used over the years but they are the core that helped build our team. Look for additional information, drills and workouts at JeffKight.com/trap-pass-move.

Chapter 7

Final Thoughts

One of the most important things to remember when coaching at young ages is that you are working with children. They don't think like adults. They don't communicate like adults. They don't have the same ambitions as adults. They want to have fun, they may want to learn but mainly they want to play.

A very important piece of advice I received when coaching u6 was *"The two most important questions to ask after a game are; Did you have fun? and What would you like to eat?"*

I don't remember where that came from but I've never forgotten it. The essence of the question is kid, the game is done let's move on. Don't try to analyze the game or your child's play (like I usually do). Just move on.

When coaching focus on the core 20% and your players will improve. As with most things 80% of a soccer match is comprised of 20% of soccer skills...**Trap – Pass – Move**. Watch Barcelona, watch Brazil, watch Real Madrid, watch Argentina or a host of other world class clubs and you will find that very few players will touch the ball more than three times per possession.

Think of that, three touches, a trap, a touch, a pass. Actually the average number of touches for a pro is closer to 2 than three. Plant the seed early in the minds of your players *"Pros don't play with the ball, they pass it."*

Remember to have fun yourself. We as adults need to let loose and remember our childlike enthusiasm for soccer and life. Stop yelling and start laughing. Train your team during practice and let them play during a game.

Coaches who constantly yell instructions to their team are doing players and themselves a disservice. Players start to relay on in-game instruction and stop thinking for themselves. A coach involved in instructing a player on a play misses the action occurring while instructing.

I have more info available at:

JeffKight.com/trap-pass-move

it's free and includes handouts I used, position explanations, dead ball instructions and more. I was a handout freak.

Allow me to Brag

(about my Team)

As I complete this book I am in my final season of coaching. This season was not planned, I had 'retired'. My team had grown, my wife was ready for less soccer in the house and we had ended a two year run at 22-4-2 which included our two previous seasons being undefeated.

More impressive to me was the progress the players had made in their personal skills and the fact that they were a TEAM.

A TEAM will defeat a group of players any day and we proved this time and time again. When we had 10 players available we played and won. The day we had eight show up we played and won. And even when there were only seven available we played and won.

No, these weren't superstars we had, they were a team that knew each other well and cared.

After that two year run I was ready to step out of the way and let the next crop of players move up and the next coach move in.

Only that didn't happen.

At the beginning of this season I received a message that there was nobody with the qualifications to coach the u14 team, would I help out.

It took two weeks for my no to turn to a yes, I'm now happy my answer changed. Not only did this give me the opportunity to coach both of my sons on the same team for the first time in many years it gave me time to test what I believe.

I was handed a roster that included; four returning players, three players who had never played soccer, eleven players with varying levels of experience moving up from u12. Yeah, a big team.

We lost our first game 2-5. As I write this we have run off five straight wins outscoring our opponents 39-2 with four consecutive shutouts.

Every single player has greatly improved his personal skills. Every player participates as a TEAM member. Every player is having fun. They are a wonderful group of kids and now a very strong team.

I may just be lucky and found a group of players who thrive with my style of coaching and my methods. These may not work for you or your players. I do strongly believe and encourage every youth soccer and futsal coach to look at and train the 20%, the core skills that comprise the majority of the game.

Running laps is a waste of time unless you practice and run 4-5 days per week or your players run for conditioning away from practice.

Dribbling drills at younger ages is unnecessary, they dribble naturally.

Having your entire team run shooting drills makes little sense, let your defenders defend and your shooters work around them to get off a shot.

Build your system around your players' skills. This season we revamped our system going from a defensive team to one focused on attack. Why? Because of the players' skill sets.

Always remind you players to **Trap – Pass – Move** and remember to HAVE FUN!

www.ingramcontent.com/pod-product-compliance
Lightning Source LLC
Chambersburg PA
CBHW062025040426
42447CB00010B/2134